Remembrance and Gratitude

Book 2

A Selection of Poems and Writings

by

Charles F. Meek

CCB Publishing
Terrace, British Columbia, Canada

Remembrance and Gratitude Book 2:
A Selection of Poems and Writings

Copyright ©2015 by Charles F. Meek
ISBN-13   978-1-77143-245-0
First Edition

Library and Archives Canada Cataloguing in Publication
Meek, Charles F., 1943-, author
Remembrance and gratitude book 2 : a selection of poems and writings /
by Charles F. Meek. -- First edition.
Issued in print and electronic formats.
ISBN 978-1-77143-245-0 (pbk.).--ISBN 978-1-77143-246-7 (pdf)
Additional cataloguing data available from Library and Archives Canada

All poems and essays contained herein are copyright Charles F. Meek.

Photos contained herein are either copyright Charles F. Meek or provided courtesy of the copyright owner.

Extreme care has been taken by the author to ensure that all information presented in this book is accurate and up to date at the time of publishing. Neither the author nor the publisher can be held responsible for any errors or omissions. Additionally, neither is any liability assumed for damages resulting from the use of the information contained herein.

All rights reserved. No part of this publication may be reproduced, stored in a retrieval system or transmitted in any form or by any means, electronic, mechanical, photocopying, recording or otherwise without the express written permission of the publisher, except by a reviewer who may quote brief passages in a review to be printed in a newspaper, magazine, or journal.

Publisher: CCB Publishing
             Terrace, British Columbia, Canada
             www.ccbpublishing.com

*This book is dedicated
in memory of*

Margaret and Bob Grier, M.B.E.

Foreword

Charles F. Meek is a man who demonstrates a selfless devotion towards his community, family, friends and even strangers in both his personal and professional life. With dignity and grace he provides comfort to those suffering and in need by showing care and respect.

I have had the pleasure of knowing Charlie only a few short years, but in that time I've come to consider him a truly great friend. He is there for you in both good times and bad, with a smile and a helpful hand.

His love and devotion to his wife Eleanor is a great joy to behold, and together they have had a long and enduring marriage filled with love and support for one another.

Through his writing Charlie remembers the good times and memorializes those who might otherwise be forgotten with touching, moving and emotional verse that truly shows his heart and spirit. I am honoured to have been able to assist him in bringing his work to readers near and far.

Paul Rabinovitch
Publisher
CCB Publishing

Praise for *Remembrance and Gratitude*

We have known Charles "Charlie" Meek almost since he arrived in Terrace. During this time he has been involved in the community in many ways, more so with the Royal Canadian Legion, Branch 13, Terrace, British Columbia.

One of the projects Charlie was involved with was in establishing Flag Poles and Memorial Markers in our two cemeteries dedicated to the veterans who are laid to rest there.

We appreciate his involvement in honoring our veterans at the time of their passing, and also for assisting our vets whilst in his position of Service Officer.

It is our pleasure to know Charlie. He certainly has a gift in his writings, as he remembers his friends, family, and places, as well as many of our friends, with prose showing love and respect.

We look forward to his visits to our home where he is always a welcome guest and interesting conversations are enjoyed. His book sits nearby and often is picked up and read with Remembrance and Gratitude.

Charlie, thank you for who you are and being there.

Helene and Bill McRae (Freeman of the City of Terrace)

Praise for *Remembrance and Gratitude*

If you were to describe someone you know in three words how would you start? Not too difficult you might think, well in this instance not really.

WORDSMITH.

Is how I would describe Charles "Charlie" Meek's talent for writing.

EMPATHY.

Is what he brings to people he meets in life and what he writes about.

COMPASSION.

For others on a daily basis.

There... done.

I've known Charlie for more years than I care to admit, and he's married to my sister Eleanor.

And although we live our lives in different parts of the world we are close friends. We see each other as often as we can in our busy lives, speaking on the phone regularly.

Since I retired from the Police Service some years ago, I now live in a small Scottish fishing village in my three hundred-year-old home, working as a furniture maker and restorer.

I often find whilst working alone in my workshop I think about the people I have had the good fortune to meet, including the Dalai Lama. People who have enriched my life and I include Charlie as one of those people.

Sean McManus
Furniture Maker and Restorer (Retired Police Officer)
Kincardine, Fifeshire, Scotland

Preface

It is with great pleasure I present to you the reader, *Remembrance and Gratitude Book 2*.

This book is dedicated to two wonderful people who were part of my wife Eleanor's and my life, Margaret and Bob Grier, M.B.E., late of Largoward, Scotland. Sadly they have both gone now, yet you can read about these two wonderful people in Book One and Two.

There are so many people I would like to thank for encouraging and inspiring me to write this second book.

First and foremost, my wife Eleanor. Helene and Bill McRae, Paul and Donna Rabinovitch from CCB Publishing, and so many more, I thank you all for your support. Also to another two wonderful people Norma and Bill Young. Thank you both.

To Sean McManus thank you for the kind words you wrote. Also to those people and businesses who supported me in selling the books, to you all I thank you, including: Thornhill Meat Market, Terrace/Kitimat Airport and Misty River Books.

I sincerely hope you enjoy the poems and writings in Book Two. Thank you all for purchasing the book, please enjoy.

Yours in Friendship,

Charlie

Contents

Foreword v
Praise for *Remembrance and Gratitude* vi
Preface ix
I Know Him Well 1
Walk With Me 2
Jack Talstra, A Legend 3
An Old Christmas Tree 4
The Smile of An Angel 5
A Clackmannan Memory 6
Clackmannan Legends 7
In A Picture Frame 8
They Are Ours 9
Stand Down Young Argyll 10
With A Heavy Heart 11
Ode to Jockey 12
Going Home 13
Deep Within 14
A New Star in Heaven 15
Tribute to Fire Chief Art Hoving (Retired) 16
My Hand in Friendship 17
Remembering Jack Alexander 18
It's Saturday Night at Largoward 19
"Jimmy" It's Been A While 20

Oh Danny Boy 21
In Loving Memory of Joy Luscombe 22
I Will Remember 23
A Prayer for Creek Bug 24
Sadness 25
I Am Nobody 26
A Forgotten Lady 27
A Golden Smile – Baby Jack 28
Two of A Kind 29
Old Tam 30
A Special Thank You 31
Some Additional Poems 32
About the Author 33

I Know Him Well

There is a man in my hometown who I know well
He is well respected, this you can tell
He is a Freeman of our city, Bill McRae is his name
His kindness and personality is his fame.

He is a veteran of a war many years ago
Although in his twilight years, he is always on the go
You see Bill is a kind man, and helpful in every way
A proud Legionnaire this I proudly say.

When you see him feel free to shake his hand
Bill McRae is a very special kind of man
Together we worked for the vets of our town
Created memorials, that will always be there and never come down.

Thank you, Bill, for being who you are. A special gentleman.

Walk With Me

Dedicated to my loving wife, Eleanor.

Do you remember, many years ago, when we were young
Walking through the glade, and the songs that we sung
Oh those days bring fond memories to me
Holding hands, and in love for everyone to see.

The years are going by, we're not as young as then
Still walking in our favourite places, we visit now and again
You take my arm, steady me on my feet
Talking to our friends we are happy to greet.

Walk with me as the years go on by
Being with you I see the lilt in your eye
Yes we are growing older the years begin to show
You will always be with me, this I do know.

So walk with me, and together we will age
Our story can be told from the very first page
Our love has been a blessing this will be told
For we will be together, as gracefully we grow old.

Thank you Carol Muir for the inspiration.

Charles F. Meek

Jack Talstra, A Legend

There is a man in our fair city, who stood proud and tall
Jack Talstra is his name, and proudly he gave his all
As a young man he became a lawyer, a lawyer well known
Jack was respected in Terrace, our hometown.

Jack came from Holland, a country far away
To Canada and Terrace, here he did stay
He was the Mayor and did this work real grand
It was a pleasure to know him, and a pleasure to shake his hand.

Jack was made a Freeman of our city, albeit for a short time
He was a special man, yes a very special kind
Now he has gone to rest, his work all finished and done
Jack is gone his memory remains, we will never see another one.

Rest in peace, Jack. Rest in peace.

An Old Christmas Tree

I still have the old Christmas from when I was a boy
Many Christmas presents, and yes the ultimate toy
To see the faces of Mum and Dad, smiles to behold
Those early days were tough times, as often we were told.

The war years were tough, Dad said presents will be under the tree
In our socks on the mantle, an apple and an orange for you and for me
And under that old tree presents and a few toys
Not just for the girls, but also the boys.

That old Christmas tree stood in the corner for many a Christmas day
Maybe we were old fashioned, I guess in our old quaint ways
We grew up and times did change, traditions always remained
Early December, decorations went up Christmas was our gain.

The old tree has now gone, but the memories have remained
That old Christmas tree, is now a photo in a picture frame
Merry Christmas, and peace be with you all
Merry Christmas.

Charles F. Meek

The Smile of An Angel

I know of a little girl with the brightest of blue eyes
Out in the snow, as she looks to the sky
It is Christmas and as excited as she could be
Looking for Santa she hopes he is near.

This little girl is quite ill, this she does not know
Her mum's and dad's wish is gracefully that she would grow
On Christmas morning her dad brought her in and sat her on his knee
Under the tree were presents she was happy to see.

Tired and weary she went for a sleep
An angel called and took her into her keep
This little girl with the brightest blue eyes
Is in heaven above, Mum and Dad can see her in the blue sky.

You see she is an angel and she looks down from above
A guardian angel to her family the ones she did love
And so every Christmas Day they look up into the skies
Looking for an angel, the one with the bright blue eyes.

A Clackmannan Memory

When I was a boy, I was a terror my mother said
I guess I was, that's why I was always early in bed
You see I liked the apples, from the minister's tree
But police man Tom Kettles he always caught me.

I loved the daffodil flowers, I gave them to my mum
She would say how lovely, then smack me on the bum
You see she knew I took them, from the garden of Mr. Gray
But Mum you can have them, you don't have to pay.

Yes I guess I was a holy terror, and only 10 years old
Climbing in Clackmannan tower to get a jackdaw, yes I was quite bold
Oh the memories of those days gone by
Now I am much older, I laugh until I cry.

I remember all our neighbours, we were all family then
Doors were unlocked, a welcome always within
Mary and Michael Barr lived in Kerse Green
Music played in the house, their home I was always seen.

Indeed a pleasant Clackmannan memory.

Charles F. Meek

Clackmannan Legends

The memories came back, from my friends across the sea
They posted online, old pictures for me to see
Many names of whom I recall
Dr. Hetherington, who always gave his all.

Crouther Gordon, our minister at the church
Stealing his apples often left me in the lurch
Then Geordie Gray, with his buses coloured green
I loved riding in them, my happiness could be seen.

From the old train station, to Miss Forsythe's wee store
Please keep passing those memories, of the years gone before
The pictures of our childhood, in black and white
Going to the gala, all dressed nice and bright.

The village of my birth, and the old miners' row
Clackmannan my home, that's where I want to go
Perhaps meet up with old friends, just for Auld Lang Syne
And sing the old Scots songs, Auld Scots Mother O' Mine.

In A Picture Frame

Darren Thomson *Alan Thomson*

On our mantle is a photo in an old picture frame
A young man stands proudly. Yes, we know his name
With a child in his arms, and medals on his chest
You see, to us, he is one of the best.

Darren is his name, baby's name is Gracie Mae
A proud father, very proud this you can see
He wears his medals, to honour all our vets
A poppy in his lapel, yes he is the best.

To all of you who read this, pay tribute to this young man
Give thanks, to his likes, he did his duty in foreign lands
Along with his brother, they fought for peace in faraway places
Alan and Darren, please remember their faces.

They are our nephews, proud we are of them.

Charles F. Meek

They Are Ours

Dedicated to our nephews
Veterans Alan and Darren Thomson

It doesn't seem so long ago that you were both little boys
Playing in the garden, playing with your toys
Then you grew up and quickly became men
Oh I remember those days, away back then.

Darren and Alan soldiers they wanted to be
Around the world strange places to see
They went to war in lands faraway
Please come home safe, we all did pray.

They saw the conflicts that war does create
Darren and Alan fought side by side with their best mates
War did take its toll and some of their friends did fall
Remember them with grandeur for they stood tall.

We are proud of our nephews they did what they had to do
They fought for their country, they fought for me and you
Stand proud young man, stand proud and be tall
We send our love to you both, we proudly give it all.

Stand Down Young Argyll

This young soldier was doing his duty this day
Standing guard at the cenotaph, head bowed as he prayed
When a lowly coward came up to him, with a gun in his hand
Fired at this soldier, took his young life, I feel so angry and sad.

With Remembrance Day not too far away
Please. Remember this fallen soldier, kneel down and pray
Give thought to his family, as they grieve this night
Pray that he is in heaven, yes, he has earned that right.

Dedicated to the memory of

Corporal Nathan Cirillo
Canadian Argyll and Sutherland Highlanders

May he rest in peace.

Charles F. Meek

With A Heavy Heart

I watched in sorrow, as they carried him shoulder high
A lone piper playing, a tear in my eye
They all came together, from all walks of life
To say goodbye to Nathan, heartbreak and strife.

Yes they carried him, they carried him shoulder high
The leaves were falling, they also seemed to cry
Canada stands proud, proud of this young man
An Argyll he was, the Argylls paid him honour, as they only can.

The lone piper played, the country came as one
They came to say goodbye, goodbye to a loving son
Let us not forget his name, Nathan, he did not die in vain
He stood in honor at the cenotaph of those gone before
Let us carve his name in stone his duty was not a chore.

As he stands down, his duty is now done
The pipes they played, for a Canadian son
Wear your poppy and wear it with pride
As we watched Nathan on his last ride.

Stand down young Argyll, stand down.

Ode to Jockey

We're here in Largoward with our kith and kin
With Aunt Margaret for a visit, she welcomed us in
Many, many years ago a blackbird came to call
Bob and Margaret called him Jockey,
his singing, they were enthralled.

They would feed him raisins, and put them on the window sill
They would call out his name, he would come and give a friendly trill
The years went on, Jockey would bring his kids,
teach them to whistle for a snack
Bob and Margaret every spring would welcome Jockey back.

I'm sure this blackbird, is a wild kind of bird
Sure he is Jockey, me thinks Jockey the 23rd
I'm sure I'll see him tomorrow, as he comes for his snack
He knows he is well off, that's why he keeps coming back.

One day I hope to see him, doing some birdy tricks
Won't surprise me if he shows up, with a white stick.

Charles F. Meek

Going Home

Largoward is in mourning, Aunt Margaret has gone
To be with Uncle Bob, that's what she had longed
You see she went to bed and fell asleep,
and left this world, but not alone
Uncle Bob he was the angel, and said,
"C'mon Lass, we're going home."

Our hearts are broken, she was so dear to us all
She is at peace, and yes she gave her all
She missed Uncle Bob, and so dearly wanted to be with him
And now they are in heaven, together with
the good Lord, they are within.

The memories we have, of those wonderful days
That we spent in Largoward, those memories will always stay
The flowers in the garden, which was Uncle Bob's joy
Aunt Margaret benefitted, that was her ploy.

Today we say a goodbye, shed a tear, from a tearful eye
She is looking down, and saying this is where I want to be
Please be happy, and listen to Billy play for Bob and me
Keep me in your prayers, the memories are yours to keep
I've closed my eyes now, I am at peace, now I sleep.

Deep Within

Loneliness is a place, a place not to be
Come share your loneliness, come share it with me
Let me be your friend, and share a friendly smile
We can walk together, down the road for a mile.

Tell me your troubles, the thoughts in your mind
Even if they are many, I will ease the troubled kind
I am here as your friend, I ask nothing in return
I offer you a friendly hand, your troubles I will burn.

Your mind will be eased, a smile upon your face
A blessing will be upon you, a blessing full of grace
Then loneliness will be gone, a memory of the past
A friendship I give to you, a friendship forever to last.

In the years to come, you will remember this day
When I offered you my hand, and took your cares away
So loneliness is a place, a place not to be
My friendship is yours to keep, this you will see.

I ask you, go on your way, to places unseen
The world is yours, go to places you have never been
Remember the friend, who gave you a helping hand
Think of yourself, of how, you now feel so grand.

Charles F. Meek

A New Star in Heaven

The day has come, the day we have dreaded
Our Jeff left with an angel, towards heaven, they were headed
He was ready and was waiting, for the sign from above
He left with a smile, and all of our love.

We knew you were leaving, and we prepared for this day
With tears in our eyes, we each had our say
We bid you a farewell, with not a dry eye
May the Lord make your journey short, through the heavenly sky.

We ask you look down upon us, as you promised to do
And when our time comes, we will come looking for you
Perhaps at the side of your favourite creek
Or standing with an angel, looking so meek.

All of us here in your second home, will miss our fun time
We will remember you, when we sing Auld Lang Syne
Now go lay down and have your earned rest
Creek we say goodbye, you are one of the best.

Rest in peace old friend, rest in peace.

C. F. Meek and all at Speedway Freaks.

Tribute to Fire Chief Art Hoving (Retired)

The year almost done, everything was going well
Sadly I ask our Chief, Chief please ring the bell
Another fireman has left us behind, has gone to join another fold
Retired Chief Hoving, a man with a heart of gold.

We will mourn his passing, and miss his friendly smile
Let us pray his journey, will take just a short while
Our thoughts and our sorrows, we share with Billie, his wife
Chief please ring the bell, we will bear the sorrow and the strife.

Chief Art was a welcome sight in our Thornhill Hall
In his teachings, his knowledge he gave it all
He will be remembered, with his name on a plaque
On our arms, a ribbon, a ribbon of black.

Even though he has left us, to join those gone before
Firemen Hill, Harris, Albright, and fireman Gerow
He left us with a legacy, of things he did do
He did them for all of us, even for me and for you.

Charles F. Meek

My Hand in Friendship

There are two people who are friends of mine
Two of the greatest, a special two of a kind
Eleanor and I are proud to know them, for what they have done
Their kids they call them, the greatest Dad, and the perfect Mum.

Many of you know Jim, a firefighter he was
From the Thornhill Fire Hall, he was a pretty good boss
He taught the firefighters to be diligent and be strong
Be careful what you do, be safe, saving lives is not wrong.

Then there is his partner, should I say in crime
Betty is a darlin, I'm proud she is a friend of mine
Betty was a nurse for many a year not too long ago
Working in Mills Memorial, saw happiness,
saw tears, and saw some go.

She looked after the sick, and took care of their ills
From everything she knew, even down to little chills
Betty and Jim are retired now, and take each day as it comes
Together they go driving, to meet new challenges,
and follow the rising sun.

Yes I am honoured to call them dear friends, and always they will be
From Eleanor and me, Jim and Betty are like us, you get what you see.

Remembering Jack Alexander

We are all in mourning, Scotland has lost a son
Jack Alexander, a man always full of fun
He had a talent, in singing with brother Tom
At the concerts, Jack would invite you to sing along.

I remember those years, which seem so long ago
When they sang here in my hometown, kilts waving to and fro
They sang in Terrace, Prince Rupert, and Vancouver as well
And down to Smithers, they were very popular, this you could tell.

We were proud to be their friends, both Eleanor and I
With this sad news, there is not a dry eye
To see Jack's casket, at the church door
Our hearts are heavy, the pain is so sore.

Even though you have gone, you are heaven's gain
Your voice will always be heard, the memories will remain
So now you join those, who have gone before
You will be welcomed, at heaven's golden door.

Heaven has a choir, musicians to play so mild
Jack will be there, to sing Nobody's Child
Rest in peace, you are heaven's gain
The memories of you, will always remain.

Charles F. Meek

It's Saturday Night at Largoward

It's Saturday night to the dancing we all go
To Largoward hall to hear the bands, and dance to and fro
The bands they travel from east and west
To Largoward where they play, and play their best.

The dancers come from far and wide, and dance for me and you
Kilts of many tartans, Greens Reds and Blues
MacDonald and MacDougal, Aye and Clan Campbell too
Look at the men and women, their kilts all a swaying
An eightsome reel or a barn dance, the band keeps on playing.

The memories I have of a Saturday night at the hall
I love to see the dancers, it's a Largoward ball
I thank you all for having me, as your guest this Saturday night
The memories of you all dancing, it is a beautiful sight.

I won't forget a man, who is very special to me
He looked after the dancing, of course
The late Bob Grier, M.B.E.

"Jimmy"
It's Been A While

Jimmy it's been a while since you have been gone
I'm often reminded when I hear a special song
When you left you never said goodbye
And yes when we heard, we broke down and cried.

That was a while ago, our hearts are starting to heal
We know you are here, your presence we do feel
We have to move on, take each day as it comes
Laugh at the silly things, yes they were fun.

I write these words Jimmy to let you know, I think of you each day
You see you were my friend, this I am proud to say
Don't think we have forgotten you, this is not so
You are always with me, always, wherever I go.

I lift my glass and toast you, my absent friend
Be my guardian angel, you were special to the very end
I pray that you are at peace, and look down from above
I am sure that you can see, that you were and you are still loved.

Charles F. Meek

Oh Danny Boy

Have you ever gone into a store and listened to what the staff may say
I do, here in my hometown at my local Safeway
You see not too long ago Danny would greet you with a smile
Maybe tell a joke and help you all the while.

Often I would go in and do some shopping there
I didn't see Danny, I didn't see him anywhere
I didn't hear the call, "Call security Charlie's here again,"
I left there today, without the laughter and the pain.

Then one evening I got a call to work, to go to someone's home
To my dismay it was Danny, the angels called him home
I took him from his home, with a tear in my eye
Danny was a friend, I didn't want him to die.

Let's not forget his humour and his cheeky smile
Danny would help you, and go the last mile
I know he retired, not too long ago
He was my friend, this I want you to know.

So each time I go into my Safeway store
I think of Danny as I walk in the door
The staff all do miss him this you will also see
He's looking down upon us, he's looking at you and me.

Rest in peace, Danny. Rest in peace.

In Loving Memory of
Joy Luscombe

You are a joy to behold, this you will often be told
Friends we will be as together we gracefully grow old
Ted is your anchor, holds you firm in all kinds of storms
His heart is of gold, his love for you is so warm.

You are our friend, a long time it has been
The friendship is true, this can be seen
Now we have learned an angel will soon call
Take you to God's great heavenly home
There you will hear the angels' choir, sing your favourite song.

There you will be at graceful peace, and look down upon us all
Be there for us in case we stumble, or even fall
The memories we have of you in our life
Are to be praised, and grateful you were Ted's loving wife.

The day has come when you went to your rest
I took you away, Joy you were one of the best
We will miss the beautiful smile and the childish grin
Peace be with you, and peace within.

Charles F. Meek

I Will Remember

Each year about this time, I prepare for Remembrance Day
I hear some people may want to take this away
I will wear my blood red poppy, and wear it with pride
I will say my prayer to Jesus, to the veterans I will abide.

On November the eleventh I will give thanks to those who fell
And listen to those who are with us, of the stories they tell
I will honour each and every one, and remember the ones I knew
Each and every year, sadly they are getting few.

Let me say, and I say it with pride,
I will remember those who have gone
On their grave, a cross, with their name carved in stone
A tribute will be paid, this Remembrance Day
To our veterans who are here, let THEM have their say.

A Prayer for Creek Bug

We all have a good friend, here on this site
At the moment he is having a bit of strife
He is in a hospital, close to his home
I wish I knew his number, I would call him on the phone.

From all of us, our thoughts and prayers are with you this day
We pray to the Lord, to let us have our say
And that is you hear our prayers, and Creek gets well soon
All of us here, would all be over the moon.

Creek stay positive fight and be strong
We need you back here, this is where you belong
From all at admin and down the members line
We are thinking of you, you WILL be back in time.

Our prayers will be heard.

Charles F. Meek

Sadness

Today we are in sadness, and with an aching heart
A dear friend has parted, he was here from the start
Many tributes have been paid, from friends here online
I am happy to say, he was a good friend of mine.

There is TPB, Oak and Aces, Kid and Jell
We are all hurting, this you can tell
Ironworks his friend, we were all there till the end
Oh how I wish our aching hearts would mend.

Even though he has gone, and left this our site
We know he fought hard to stay, he fought with all his might
Many names I haven't mentioned, you know who you are
Look up into the heavens you will see a bright new star.

Let us all, each and everyone,
say a silent prayer, for our lost loved one
When he was on site, everyone had laughter and fun
His voice is now silent, his heart beats no more
His eyes have gone dim, he will no longer walk the floor.

Yes, our hearts are aching, our eyes filled with tears
We know where you are, there is no more fear
Be at peace, you have earned your rest
Jeff, you were one of the best.

I Am Nobody

I am nobody, you can't see me, but I can see you
Wherever you go, I will go too
I was there when you were given life
Right through the years, to when you took a wife.

To your friends you never acknowledge that I was there
I stood by you, through thick and thin, I was always there
But I am nobody, you can't see me, I am there for you
All the things you do, I do with you.

I am there to share the joy and laughter together
Even sadness, I am there, in all kinds of weather
And when you go to sleep at night
I am there, just to your right.

But you can see me, the days that you are having fun
Those are the days, when in the sky is the bright sun
One day you will find me, this I know
For you see, I am, your shadow.

Charles F. Meek

A Forgotten Lady

She was just an old lady in an old folks' home
Nobody came to visit, nobody bothered to phone
She was cared for by the staff, who looked after her needs
That's what they do in Terraceview, their work is in their deeds.

Nobody came to visit, nobody bothered to phone
Once she was a mother, and had a beautiful home
Her husband passed away, the kids grew up and moved to other places
She became forgetful, couldn't remember faces.

She needed to be cared for, she couldn't look after herself
She felt like an old book, forgotten and put on a shelf
This dear old lady had a heart of gold
Her only problem in life, was that she grew old.

It saddens me to hear this, she passed away all alone
Nobody asked about her, nobody bothered to phone
I spoke at her funeral, prayed for her to be at rest
She just wasn't an old lady, to me she was one of the best.

Nobody came to visit, nobody bothered to phone.

A Golden Smile
Baby Jack

You came into this world, with a smile on your face
We looked at you lovingly, you were so full of grace
We knew within our hearts that you were only on loan
It would have been our joy to bring you to your home.

We named you Jack from your grandfather before
I wanted to cradle you in my arms, and walk with you on the floor
This was not to be for an angel in heaven is where you will be
I know I can look up to the stars and your sweet face I will see.

Mum and Dad do love you, this will always be
Our hearts they are breaking, this you can see
The angels in heaven were waiting, waiting for you to come
We had to let you go, this we did, your dad and your mum.

We will sit together, your dad and I mention your sweet name
Of how we had you, now you're the good Lord's gain
I hear the angels' choir, I hear them singing above
They are singing for you, Jack, our son our darling love.

Dedicated to the memory of Baby Jack
March 5th to March 20th 2015

Charles F. Meek

Two of A Kind

Dedicated to Gordon and Carol Muir

I've met many people from all walks of life
In doing things I do, I take it all in stride
Then we met some people, we do things for to no end
These special people have become lifelong friends.

You see this friendship such as ours, cannot be bought
The friendship is earned and yours we have got
To Gordon and Carol, we are always here to lending a helping hand
As you were when I needed you, you took a friendship stand.

True friendship is lifelong, no matter where we roam
Our door is always open, a place you can call home
You both are very special, a big part of our life
True friendship for always to me and to my wife.

Old Tam

Old Tam was a horse who pulled the milkman's cart
Not just a horse, a Clydesdale with a lot of heart
You could see him working each and every day
Give him a treat he would gently go on his way.

Some days it would be coal, maybe milk or a beer dray
Ay'e Old Tam was a wonder his owner would say
At the end of the day in the field he would run
Acting like a foal galloping for fun.

Ay'e Old Tam was well known in our town
Give him an apple, rarely he would frown
Then Old Tam retired a big van took his place
We missed seeing him, kisses and slobbering on our face.

Old Tam he is gone now these many years ago
You can still hear the clip clop as he goes to and fro
Ay'e those were the days when being a boy was fun
Playing in the field with Old Tam and seeing him run.

Giddy up, Tam, giddy up.

Charles F. Meek

A Special Thank You

You say you love my writings, and the words that I have wrote
Many of them are true, and to many I have spoke
I like to feel that you are with me, and live the words I write
Of the people who are dedicated, I think of them at night.

Many of the works, are of people, people who have gone
And yet I remember, each and every one
It is my way of remembering, a friendship I do miss
To the heavens I look, and blow them a nightly kiss.

I am pleased you enjoy, and understand what I say
Often of faraway places, places far away
To the land of my birth, where once I walked the land
I give you my hand in friendship, I ask you take my hand.

In years to come, when the Good Lord calls
I leave my words, to remember me by, I leave them to you all
I give thanks, to you, who have thanked me
My thanks to you, are in my writings for you to see.

If I can make someone happy, and a smile on their face
Your thoughts and comments, are so full of grace
I am your dear friend, and I am who I am
I will keep on writing, as long as I can.

Some Additional Poems

I hope you have enjoyed the poems and writings in the book. As you have read, I often officiate at funerals and memorial services for our veterans, and members of my branch at the Royal Canadian Legion, as well as for Remembrance Day services.

There are some poems I read at those services, even though I did not write them myself. The words of these poems accent the service. I have listed some of these poems below and provided a link so you may read them and enjoy their meanings.

When Tomorrow Starts Without Me
http://www.poeticexpressions.co.uk/POEMS/Iftomorrowstartswithoutme.htm

Letter from Heaven
http://unforgettableangels.angelstouch16.com/Letter/letter.htm

My First Christmas in Heaven
http://www.utahshare.org/newsletter/2012/11/01/1051/

The Old Comrade
http://www.rcl462.ca/old-comrade.html

Why Wear A Poppy
http://www.veterans.gc.ca/eng/feature/vetweek/comm_guide/poems

Merry Christmas, My Friend
http://www.hymnsandcarolsofchristmas.com/Poetry/merry_christmas_my_friend.htm

Just A Common Soldier
http://vaincourt.homestead.com/common_soldier.html

Sincerely yours,
Charlie

About the Author

Charles F. Meek has lived in Terrace, British Columbia ever since emigrating from Scotland in 1979. He is very involved in his community. Over the years he has been Commanding Officer of 747 Squadron of the local Air Cadets and past President of Royal Canadian Legion Branch 13.

Working for the veterans was first and foremost, and he still hosts the Remembrance Day services from the Tillicum Twin Theatres on November 11th of each year, which is broadcast on CityWest's Community Channel 10. He has also hosted a Scottish radio show, *A Touch O' White Heather*, and television program, *Down in the Glen*. At one time Charlie was a Marriage Commissioner. He enjoyed seeing many happy people and has many fond memories.

Assisting others is a part of his life, and he continues helping people by serving at funeral and memorial services. Now semi-retired, Charlie enjoys fishing on the ocean with friends. Charlie is married to his wife Eleanor, who has inspired many of his poems and writings.

www.ingramcontent.com/pod-product-compliance
Lightning Source LLC
Chambersburg PA
CBHW031659040426
42453CB00006B/346